T0157261

LEAVING LIBERTY?
Essays on Politics and Free-Market Thinking

Martin Mazorra

iUniverse, Inc.
Bloomington

iUniverse books may be ordered through booksellers or by contacting:

iUniverse
1663 Liberty Drive
Bloomington, IN 47403
www.iuniverse.com
1-800-Authors (1-800-288-4677)

ISBN: 978-1-4759-7044-9 (sc)
ISBN: 978-1-4759-7045-6 (e)

Library of Congress Control Number: 2013900061

Printed in the United States of America

iUniverse rev. date: 3/25/2013

To Judy, my love!

TABLE OF CONTENTS

PREFACE

I must have well over a dozen untouched books strewn throughout my home and office. A reference made by a respected economist and I'm instantly off to load my Amazon. com shopping cart. The thing is, after my family, my day job (investment consultant), my blog, and a little exercise, staring down the spine of a three-inch-thick hardcover on the economy of the lost continent of Mu (as inviting and relevant as that sounds) all too often leaves me resigned to skimming the online edition of the *Times* or the *Wall Street Journal*. I do love to read, mind you; it's just that there are times when my brain cells aren't firing at a level that will do justice to a book like *An Inquiry into the Nature and Causes of the Wealth of Nations* or *The General Theory of Employment, Interest, and Money.* Every now and then I just need a quick fix. Something short, something easy to take in—and I'm guessing you can relate.

You therefore hold in your hands the quickest of fixes—although that's not how it began. This brief exposé was a mere editing away from becoming chapter 1 of a thought-provoking, can't-put-down, life-changing kind of book (or so I was dreaming) on the global economy and the markets. But thankfully, somewhere between page 592 and the epilogue, I woke up. I mean if I'm reluctant to dive into something as tantalizing as *The Economy of Mu*, why would I expect you to commit untold hours to a study of politics, class warfare, international trade, taxes, investing, and the global economy?

You're thus staring down the thinnest and most inviting of spines: a daily devotional collection of my select essays on politics and the economy.

I aim to touch a nerve. To get you thinking about where today's politician, left to his own devices, might lead us. To impress upon you that allowing the marketplace to work, unfettered (as possible) by government, is the way we get America back on track. This book allows you to take it slow: one essay, one day at a time, for thirty-one days. Or, if you prefer, and brain cells permitting, you can knock the whole thing out in one sitting. Again, my objective is to enlighten you—to bring you, in straightforward fashion, to a free-market way of thinking.

INTRODUCTION

Wall Street fascinates me—the market, the auction process, the myriad ways investors and traders approach the business of speculation. Your old-school financial adviser, the buy-and-hold enthusiast, would tell you that for long holding periods, a diversified portfolio of stocks involves minimal speculation, and that short-term trading is speculation by definition. While his intent would be noble, and not completely amiss, since long-term buy-and-hold investing has historically lessened one's odds of losing in the market, it nevertheless involves a great deal of speculation. Speculating on whether to do it yourself or hire an adviser. Speculating on whether your adviser is to be trusted and whether she knows her stuff. Speculating on whether demographic and political trends will favor your chosen strategy. Speculating on whether you're investing enough to retire at the age you desire. And speculating on the notion that capitalism will survive the pendulum's momentum that has—in at least one very large economy, some believe—recently swung toward a collectivist mind-set.

Speaking of such mind-sets, politics, as we'll explore, can impact consumer sentiment like nothing you've ever seen—and today's (and yesterday's, for that matter) incumbent knows this all too well. He's fully aware that the economy will ultimately determine the result of his reelection bid. Thus, when we're in the contraction phase of the cycle, he'll desperately assign blame to the other side of the aisle, with his finger pointing firmly at his predecessor. Conversely, when we're expanding, he'll take all the credit.

Today's conservative rails against the current "liberal" administration—bemoaning bailouts and stimulus packages that have thus far, they say, only stimulated our nation's burgeoning deficits. Now where were these conservatives when, under a Republican regime, the Fed, led by a Republican-appointed chairman, took monetary stimulus to a new extreme—and seeded what became the mother of all real estate bubbles? Where were these conservatives when, under their watch, the present bailout craze was born?

And what of today's so-called liberal? He rails against the supposed grip certain organizations have on the Republican Party, while turning a blind eye to his own party's blatant bias for numerous special interests, not the least of which is unions.

We're three-plus years into the Obama administration, and Bush is still held culpable for everything "bad" happening today. Dear old Ronald Reagan, well into his first term, leveraged Jimmy Carter's tattered rep ad nauseam when things weren't progressing as rapidly as he had hoped. Now, if you're a devoted Democrat, you'd say, "Absolutely, it is Bush's fault. Obama's just telling the truth." If you're a staunch Republican, you insist that "Obama is indeed screwing things up royally, and all he can do is blame Bush." Alas, while it's disgustingly apparent that intellectual honesty is an extinct commodity in

Washington, recognizing its lack in ourselves is an altogether different proposition.

Please, therefore, try to suspend your preconceptions as you read on.

Note: Where I deemed an essay to be time sensitive, I either point to a date within the body of the text or include the month and year next to the title.

DAY 1:
The Good Old Days

When I look to the future I get very nervous,
but when I look to the past I feel pretty good.
—James Buchanan (Buchanan)

I'm generally not one for reminiscing, but the other day I found myself in the throes of a sentimental moment. A friend forwarded me an e-mail titled *To Those of Us Born 1925–1970*, and man did it ever take me back. Back to my childhood, to a simpler time, to a time when kids could entertain themselves for hours on end—without the luxuries of video games or cable television. I literally got goose bumps as I was reminded of how my pals and I would pile into the backs of our parents' pickups after Little League games. But now that I think about it, I'm not entirely sure whether my goose bumps were inspired by nostalgia or by my memories of how friggin' cold it was riding in the back of a truck.

Ah, the good old days, when the future seemed so bright! Like during the Great Depression, WWII, Korea, Vietnam, the Cuban missile crisis, Kennedy's assassination, Nixon's resignation, the Arab oil embargo (remember those gas lines?), the Cold War, 19 percent mortgage rates, the junk bond scandal, the savings and loan crisis, the Mexican and Asian currency crises, the 1987 stock market crash, the bursting of the tech bubble, September 11, 2001, the bursting of the real estate bubble, and the myriad events between all those I just listed? Seriously, if you were born between 1925 and 1970—or from 1970 on, for that matter—how often were you truly looking to the future with optimism?

In the words of economist James Buchanan, "When I look to the future I get very nervous, but when I look to the past I feel pretty good."

Now in spite of my calamitous chronology, I believe those of us born in the heart of the twentieth century indeed have much to be thankful for. Life was blissfully less complicated back when the notion of paying even a nickel (let alone a buck-fifty) for a bottle of water, as we drank from garden hoses, would have seemed utterly absurd. Yet while we will forever romanticize our past, we nonetheless strive mightily to make life more comfortable for ourselves and for our posterity. And clearly we have succeeded beyond our wildest expectations.

Pessimists consider themselves realists, and they call optimists idealists. But like Buchanan, when I look to the past and consider how far we've come, I'm thinking the optimists had it right.

Of course we have issues. We've always had issues, and of course we always will. You may indeed be pessimistic—you indeed have reason to be—and you'll indeed be proven right every now and again. Or you may be an optimist; you indeed have reason to be, and you'll indeed be proven right every now and again as well.

I've often wondered if we even have a choice, in terms of our tendency toward one or the other. Perhaps it's a chemical thing, or maybe it's environmental. Speaking for myself, particularly when we're talking public policy, I concede to both. But again, when I look at the world in retrospect, when my thinking transcends the headlines of the day, I can't help but be optimistic in the long run.

If you consider yourself a "realist," no offense—I did not intend here to criticize you. For as the buyer needs the seller, you are every bit as essential to the market's function as the optimist.

Or, for that matter, if you're an optimist, I did not intend here to inflate your ego. For you are the pessimist's pawn. When Gloomy Gus gets it right, there has to be some bleary-eyed buyer to sell to.

DAY 2:
The Fishermen Are Sleeping In
(August 2012)

A stagnant pond simply cannot sustain the type of fish you and I would bring home for supper.

On most Thursday mornings, beginning in May and ending sometime midsummer of each year, a Department of Fish and Game tanker loaded with dozens of squirmy eight- to fourteen-inch rainbow trout pulls up to a tiny reservoir about an hour's drive north of Fresno and sets them free. Although I'm not sure "free" is an apt description of a trout's existence in what amounts to an oversized moss-infested pond, where only the heartiest of carp and a few catfish will survive the blistering heat of the coming August.

So why would the California Department of Fish and Game do such a thing? While I've yet to explore the economics of trout-planting—although we're talking government, so it wouldn't be pretty anyway—it obviously has something to do with fishermen. Those men's men who—rather than sleeping in like city folk and later visiting the corner grocer to snatch the protein for the evening's supper—will rise with the roosters; pack their trunks with rods, reels, and split-shot sinkers; and venture off to test their angling skills (and a fresh jar of glow-in-the-dark bait that smells just like the fish food at the hatchery) on the unwary salmonoids …

It is no doubt in the Department's best interest, for whatever reason, to cater to the animal spirits of the Central California angler. To get him out of the recliner and into the sporting goods store to purchase the government-issued license along with all the necessary tackle. And/or perhaps to send out a game warden to lie in waiting behind a pond-shore bush in hopes of surprising the cheater who skipped the licensing part, and slapping him with a $400 (no kidding) fine.

We'll call it a staging—an artificial catering to man's primal urge to bear the wilds, to take the risks necessary to provide for his family. But, alas, while most vivid on Thursdays, this grand illusion fades by Sunday. And by the time Wednesday rolls back around, the returning gentleman, now with six grandkids in tow—anticipating another day of great fishing—drives away empty-ice-chested and bewildered, indeed uninspired to return. The simple fact is that a stagnant pond cannot sustain the type of fish you and I would bring home for supper.

Now let's think in terms of fiscal and monetary stimulus. The economy's barely moving, and rather than clearing the muck and allowing the flow of fresh current, our "leaders" have been further damming the pond with new regulations and the threat of higher taxes. It's like expecting folks to come fishing when the pond is choked with moss and the DFG just doubled the price of a license. Washington can toss in one-time incentives (*Cash for Clunkers*, *Homebuyers Tax Credits*, and the like) and the Fed can plant billions a month till the cows come home, but until they pull the garbage (newly adopted and threatened policies) out of the back end of the pond, the fishermen, I'm afraid, are sleeping in.

DAY 3:

Free to Lose

*I say we let markets, as opposed
to politicians, deal with risk.*

"The major revelation of the last four years was the fragility
of the global economy," European Central Bank President
Jean-Claude Trichet said on July 10, 2011. "Strengthening
resilience is absolutely essential given the fragility exhibited by
the global economy." He called for a "serious advance in the
way we regulate systemic institutions, including nonbanking
institutions" (Market Watch, 2011).

Europe's policymakers, like ours, are desperate to convince
the people that government owns no culpability (save for too-
light regulations) for the credit crisis and is indeed the white
knight who will not only save the day but save us from ourselves
in the years to come.

So is that the answer? Do we need a "serious advance"
by government? Do we need bureaucrats to exert yet more
influence on business, to determine the dos and don'ts,

the rights and wrongs? Do we need government to set the boundaries, while checking creativity in the process? Is that how we become better, stronger, safer even?

Name me a single government-sponsored endeavor that you would honestly deem a financial success. Can't think of any? How about the Troubled Asset Relief Program (TARP)—a.k.a. the Banking (and ultimately the Auto) Industry Bailout? Which has thus far netted the taxpayer a profit (on its investment in banks)—a heavily disputed claim made by Treasury Secretary Timothy Geithner (US Treasury Press Center, 2011). So perhaps that's an example of government policy gone good, right? Well, I'm skeptical. There's always the counterfactual: might we be even better off had we allowed failed institutions to fail, had we let the markets clear and purge the excesses (and teach the all-important lessons) born of the last expansion?

Consider the 2008 real estate/mortgage backed securities bubble and the once-revered tenure of Alan Greenspan. There was a time when the maestro's playing of the printing press in response to the 2002 recession was deemed one of history's great monetary policy achievements. Today's consensus, however, is that the 2008 bubble would not have occurred had it not been for Greenspan's overfertilizing the financial sector. He also manned the helm of the late-twentieth-century bailouts that I suspect inspired the unbridled risk-taking that led to the mortgage crisis—a new round of moral hazarding that the likes of Mr. Trichet, Christopher Dodd, and Barney Frank would lever to bring a whole new slew of stifling regulations to bear on the financial sector.

In my passionate opinion, the last thing we need is more government. I say we let markets, as opposed to politicians, deal with risk—leaving investors and entrepreneurs to their own devices. That is, let's leave them free to win, on their own terms, and thus—most importantly—free to lose.

DAY 4:
The Politician's Nature

Beware the politician who promises he can fix everything.

"If few people in the Western world now want to remake society from the bottom according to some ideal blueprint, a great many still believe in measures which, though not designed completely to remodel the economy, in their aggregate may well unintentionally produce this result." —F. A. Hayek

It is the nature of the politician—intentions notwithstanding—to attempt to fix the things that bring pain to his constituents. Like the overprotective parents who can't bear to witness their child suffering the normal pains of life, who carefully arrange the child's experiences, who provide for every whim, who fill life's potholes before the little angel can lose a step, and who ultimately deliver an emotionally anemic adult void of any real-life problem-solving skills. One who sees government (as he did Mommy and Daddy) as the answer to all the world's challenges. This surely describes the incubation of many of today's politicians.

Thus, when the economic cycle inevitably turns and the excesses born of every expansion unwind and create unavoidable pain, beware the politician who promises he can fix everything, claiming he can allay all future pain and risk through legislation and tighter regulation. In other words: can you spell bailout, national healthcare, financial industry regulatory reform (FINREG), etc.? All these are, perhaps, worthy pursuits individually and in their intent, but as Hayek suggested, in their aggregate they may well unintentionally produce an undesirable result.

DAY 5:
I'll Pass, but Thanks Anyway (October 2012)

You can't help me without hurting my prospects for helping myself.

Mitt Romney promises to help me and my family. President Obama and company promise to help me, my family, my union, my waistline, my kids' test scores, my fuel efficiency, my you-name-it. To both gentlemen I say, "I'll pass, but thanks anyway."

"Why?" they ask.

"Because I understand what you assume I don't—that you can't help me without hurting someone else in the process. What you would give me and my family you would have to take from someone else and his family. In fact, you can't help me without hurting my prospects for helping myself. For when you help me—and extract resources from those who are helping themselves—you weaken the very fabric of our economy. And, worst of all, you rob me of my ability to fend for myself—not only by limiting my opportunities but, worse yet, by instilling in me a welfare mind-set."

DAY 6:
Let's Hope Our Grandkids Are the Forgiving Sort

*Prudence, alas, is lost on tomorrow's—
and other people's—money.*

So the present administration throws a few billion at solar companies. They say we're investing in the future: the future of the energy industry, future jobs, and the future of this planet. Therefore—given high unemployment, rising oil prices, and melting ice caps—it's worth every dollar "we" can throw at it.

Breaking news! As I type this in April of 2012, First Solar, the nation's largest and heavily government-subsidized solar company, just announced that it will cut its workforce by 30 percent to align its operations more closely with current opportunities. Its stock is up 6 percent to $22.05 per share on the news. Incidentally, it traded north of $120 just a year ago—but hey, we're thinking long-term.

Now you and I know that all government spending is

taxpayer funded—so, being that we are a long way from running a surplus, why haven't these "investments" required an immediate increase in our income taxes? Well, as a practical matter, had the powers-that-promote-green-power forced a tax hike to fund these grand "investments," we voters would be none too friendly come this November. So then, alas, they borrow. For they know that us consumers will allow the worst sort of chicanery when we're given thirty years to pay for it (let's hope our grandkids are the forgiving sort).

That's why the costs of proposed schemes are forever fed to us in ten-year servings: "The Congressional Budget Office estimates that the cost of XYZ over the next ten years will be $X," or "Over the next ten years the deficit will be reduced by $X if we raise taxes on people who earn above $Y." Sound familiar? Prudence, alas, is lost on tomorrow's—and other people's—money.

DAY 7:

Dude, We Need to Put You on a Diet (November 2011)

Dudes, we have to cut spending.

There's this raging debate, with regard to the federal budget deficit, shaking the walls of our nation's capitol—one side argues for spending cuts, the other for tax increases. Let's see how the arguments stack up against a little everyday commonsense.

So the nurse invites you back and asks you to slip off your four-inch-heel boots. You step on the scale, she rests the sliding bar on 261 pounds, you cheat a tiptoe to 59 inches.

Ninety minutes later (you're starving), the doc says, "Dude, we need to put you on a diet!"

You ask, "How about diet pills?"

Doc says, "No, I don't like the side effects, and your heart's not sounding so good. Let's see how you do with just cutting calories for a while."

You say, "No way, Doc! That's not fair! If you don't give me the pills I'm not cutting back on what I eat!"

"What're you nuts?" cries Doc. "Whether or not you get the pills, assuming you wanna live, you still gotta go on a diet!"

Now let's look at the same scenario, but with a different, less sensible, doctor, and a more sensible you.

The doc enters the room and says, "Dude, we need to write you a prescription."

You elatedly ask, "You mean I don't have to diet?"

Doc says, "Nope. We have a drug that will stimulate your metabolism and get you in shape without you changing a thing."

"I love it!" you cry. "But it sounds too good to be true. Are there any side effects?"

Doc says, "Well, I'm going to have to prescribe a pretty high dose, so there's no guarantee. But don't sweat it. We'll wean you off at just the right time, and at just the right pace, so you'll be fine."

You ask, "So it's not addictive?"

Doc says, "Well, it can be. That's why we'll have to wean you off slowly."

You deflatedly ask, "But once I'm off the medicine, if I haven't changed my lifestyle, won't I end up in the same mess, maybe worse, down the road?"

"What're you nuts?" cries Doc. "I have a solution that will get you back in shape now without you cutting a thing, and you're worried about what might happen years from now?"

So our nation's frame currently supports $2.2 trillion

(revenue) per year. We step on the scale and we're at $3.7 trillion (spending). One side says, "Dudes, we have to cut spending!" while the other says, "How about we raise taxes and pump up the stimulus spending?" The one side says, "Let's see how we do with just spending cuts first, and let the market work." The other says, "That's not fair! If you don't give us tax, and targeted spending, increases, we're not cutting a dime!"

Crazy!

Now we can only wish that those on the cut-spending side would be true in their pursuit. But, sadly, when it comes to cutting aid (subsidies, etc.) to their supporters, I suspect they'll have none of it

DAY 8:
Makes Me Nervous
(March 2012)

Will we save in the long run by spending more in the short run?

The following, from this morning's *New York Times* article "A Moment of Truth for Health Care Reform" (Boffey, 2012), caught my attention: "The critics insist that the mandate is unconstitutional because it regulates inaction. But the distinction they draw between inaction and action makes little sense. Refusing to pay a tax, for instance, is 'inaction' that is clearly subject to government regulation. Choosing not to have health insurance is just as clearly a financial action—one that could shift future medical expenses onto others in the health system."

So by forcing individuals to carry medical insurance (private or public) we circumvent "the shift of one's medical expenses onto others in the health system." Really? Now I certainly don't have the answers to "our" health care problems, but I do know who pays for public programs. And I know who pays when insurance companies are forced to cover individuals they wouldn't otherwise cover.

And what then will we do about the gentleman who sits at Mickeydee's drive-thru window in his idling Oldsmobile, spewing exhaust fumes into the lungs of the children eating McNuggets and guzzling Cherry Cokes in Ronald's playground, as he, after flicking the unfiltered Camel butt into the flowerbed, orders two Big Macs, a large order of fries, three hot apple pies, and a large vanilla shake? Do you think maybe his actions (not to mention the actions of the parents of the nugget-stuffed kids) will put a little pressure on "our" health care system? If the regulating of inaction is indeed ruled constitutional, we'll then have no problem regulating this man's choice of automobile, his nicotine intake, and his food. For "clearly these are financial actions—ones that could shift future medical expenses onto others"—with or without health care reform. Imagine the headline: "A Moment of Truth for the Personal Choices Reform Act."

You may be a fan of the Affordable Care Act, and you may have it right—as I said, I don't have the answers. The fiscal question is will this intervention ultimately produce the savings the Congressional Budget Office projects over the next ten years? That is, will we save in the long run by spending more in the short run? The moral question is do we continue to allow tens of millions of Americans to go without health coverage? Of course some would say the moral question is do we force hundreds of millions of Americans to pay for the tens of millions who go without health coverage? Yes, I know; they already do (those-who-can pay more to compensate for the care provided to those-who-can't). And at what point, in the interest of the greater good, do we force some bureaucrat's idealized lifestyle onto ourselves? Ridiculous? Let's hope so.

As for me, I'm a fan of freedom, and this one makes me nervous.

DAY 9:
The Market at Work
(November 2011)

Corporations themselves are inanimate objects.

According to this morning's headlines, Bank of America will announce today that it will drop its plan to charge some customers five dollars a month for debit card purchases. This follows similar moves by the competition.

No legislation, no new regulation—just the market at work. Customers spoke with their feet, credit unions grabbed some new business, and the big banks decided that hitting their customers in this fashion wasn't in their best interest after all.

Now before you get too excited, understand that legislation did intrude on the marketplace with the Durbin Amendment, which effectively cut (by 50 percent) the per-swipe fee charged to merchants. This cost the likes of Bank of America's shareholders, employees, and customers some $2 billion a year (Sanati, 2012). Notice I said *shareholders, employees, and customers*—that's who pays corporate expenses. Corporations themselves are inanimate objects.

The question now is how will shareholders, employees, and customers share the pain inflicted by the Durbin Amendment? Lower deposit rates, higher loan fees, maybe? I wonder if the *amendment* won't ultimately cost the customer *more* than $5 a month.

Well, guess what! Just three weeks later, a *New York Times* headline reads, Banks Quietly Ramping Up Costs to Consumers (Dash 2012). See!

DAY 10:
Germ-Free—Or, How Not to Become a Five Handicap—Or, Who the Hell Is Goethe?

Character is formed in the stormy billows of the world.
—Goethe

Whether we're talking the politician with no business experience or the equally sheltered PhD Fed chairman, I'm thinking that the follies of public policy we free-market types like to point out have much to do with the fact that today's policymakers (so many of them) were reared in an essentially academic environment. It's like that immune system study where a group of chickens were grown in an optimally comfortable environment: perfect temperature, plenty of the best feed, no risk or challenges whatsoever. After a few generations the scientists placed the offspring of these chickens in a normal environment. They all quickly died.

Or, using a sports analogy: it's like believing that listening to Bob Rotella tapes, without ever visiting the driving range, will make you a five handicap. It's like, with flying colors, passing every written test on the golf swing, earning a PhD in golf even, and then, in horror, totally missing the ball while attempting your first drive off the first tee.

I think I'll write a novel about a successful businessman turned policymaker. Imagine the cocktail party with the Board of Governors of the Federal Reserve: "My good man," says the governor when the topic turns to inflation, "in the words of Goethe, all things are only transitory." Not knowing (and wondering how the hell you spell) Goethe, the academically challenged appointee unashamedly asks, "Who?" Upon enlightening his intellectual subordinate in condescending, doctoratesque fashion, the Harvard valedictorian is taken aback by the seeming arrogance in his underling's nod and grin—as if he was saying, "Just testing you, my good man" or "I don't waste my time on nineteenth-century German literature" or "while you spent your youth nose-crammed in the crack of a book, and a professor's ass, I was conducting business in the real world."

In other words, in the words of Johann Wolfgang Von Goethe, "Character is formed in the stormy billows of the world."

DAY 11:

Brains to Burn
(November 2010)

*The economy is cyclical, and all the braniacs on
the planet can't do anything about it.*

In their book *Freakonomics*, the rather curious duo of Steven
Levitt, an economist, and Stephen Dubner, a journalist, tell us
"why conventional wisdom is so often wrong. How 'experts'
bend the facts. Why knowing what to measure, and how to
measure it, is the key to understanding modern life." They pose,
then unravel, a number of life's great mysteries, including why
drug dealers still live with their mothers, what sumo wrestlers
and schoolteachers have in common, and whether children
reared in homes with more books do better in school than
children who come from homes without books. I personally
have been contemplating writing an essay titled, **"What Do
Drug Dealers and Politicians Have In Common?"** but I'll save
that for another day.

I found the childhood aptitude study particularly

fascinating. As it turns out, there exists a definite correlation between books in the home and children's test results—the more the books, the better the scores. What's fascinating is that whether or not the kids with the books ever crack one has absolutely nothing to do with anything. In fact, in the featured example, the book-rich kid, who scored the highest, never read any—while the bookless child, who scored the lowest, spent every afternoon at the library reading voraciously. So what gives? Well, I hate to say it, but, according to the authors, it's all about genetics. The fact is that homes with crammed bookshelves tend to house parents with crammed craniums. And a high IQ, they conclude, is a function of breeding, as opposed to parenting—that is, a child's capacity for test-taking hinges on her genes, not her thirst, or lack thereof, for learning.

The good news is that those of us who lack PhD-worthy (without monumental effort) quotients need not fret over our genetically compromised youngsters. For, contrary to what I'm certain the genius parents themselves think, there exists no correlation between a 4.0 GPA and ultimate success in life. I might go so far as to argue that the child who has to strain to keep up stands to develop a work ethic that would contribute substantially more to his or her prospects for later success, versus that of the genetically endowed child to whom things come easy. Sounds good anyway.

You name him/her: Alan Greenspan, Ben Bernanke, Lawrence Summers, Christine Romer, Austin Goolsby, and so on. If there's one constant among the individuals who've been appointed to either rule monetary policy (as in the case of Fedheads Bernanke and Greenspan) or advise our leaders on fiscal policy (Summers, Romer, and Goolsby), it's that they're all off the bloody charts when it comes to IQs. Just Google any one of these names and you'll see academic achievements that'll blow your easily boggled mind—they were simply born with brains to burn. And thus, whenever I'm inclined to critique one of these geniuses, given my academic dearth, I stop and ask myself, "How can I even pretend to criticize an individual whose intellect easily runs circles around mine?" But then again, if academic prowess is all Washington needs to make sound financial policy, how do we find ourselves facing a 1.4+ trillion dollar budget deficit come 2011? My business ain't runnin no deficit.

Here's the thing: the economy is cyclical, and all the brainiacs on the planet can't do anything about it. The Fed, for example, has a dual mandate of *price stability and full employment*, which, by political design (Congress added the "full employment" mandate in 1977), doesn't leave much room for cyclicality— recessions are death knells to political careers. Yes, inflation is, per Milton Friedman, a monetary phenomenon. But never mind what might result from turning over-indulgent politicians loose on eager-to-please Fed officials—from tilting Fed policy (opening the monetary floodgates that is) toward influencing the hiring decisions of business owners and the voting decisions of consumers. I mean the housing bubble wasn't so bad, was it?

And, besides, if we presume that accommodative monetary policy can directly, positively, impact employment (which recent history makes a very questionable presumption), what happens when it's time for the Fed to ease off on all that easy money? At best, temporary measures yield temporary results.

The sad thing is, we average-IQ'd consumers, knowing our limitations, blindly accept the notions proffered by these appointed geniuses. And, worse yet, we may even advocate for a given program when we've been led to believe that it would benefit us directly—regardless of its defiance of what we know to be fiscally prudent.

DAY 12:

Billions to the Wind
(May 2012)

*Nothing inspires prudence like suffering
a loss every now and again.*

Jamie Dimon's on the hot seat over some $2 billion (and counting) in recent losses on derivatives, fueling the fire for those pushing for yet more regulation of the financial industry. We're talking about JP Morgan, the firm that had the wherewithal to take over Bear Stearns and Washington Mutual (with a little help from the Fed) during the 2008 credit crisis—the firm that has earned over $4 billion a quarter over the past couple of years, the firm with $2.3 trillion in assets and $190 billion in shareholder equity, for crying out loud.

Now wouldn't you think that a firm with the ability to generate some $19 billion in earnings in a given year (last year) is taking on a little risk here and there? Indeed, without that four-letter-word, could a firm even begin to generate that kind of cash? But, alas, we're talking about a big, systemically important bank. What's to keep its people from making similar mistakes going forward, which cumulatively could indeed threaten the system once again? Don't we therefore need to regulate away that sort of behavior? Nope. For there is yet another four-letter concept that offers all the incentive bankers need to better calculate their bets. It's something we call *loss*. Something our officials just can't bring themselves to allow when it comes to the big banks (save for Lehman, but my how they tried). Believe me, nothing inspires prudence like suffering a loss every now and again. Creating yet more regulations (that is, growing the size of government), on the other hand, inspires lobbying, cronyism and, sadly, outright corruption.

All that said, there is this other firm that I'm thinking we do indeed need to clamp down on—big time. This one's upside-down by $16 trillion and burning another $1.5 trillion a year (talk about systemic relevance!). Yet, puzzlingly, its top execs hypocrites were quoted recently as saying things like, "The enormous loss JPMorgan announced today is just the latest evidence that what banks call 'hedges' are often risky bets that so-called 'too big to fail' banks have no business making." (Reuters, 2012) Those would be the comments of none other than Senator Carl Levin. I'm thinking the good senator ought to concern himself with the billions he and his team are throwing to the wind, or the sun (as it were), on "risky bets" like Solyndra, and let Mr. Dimon deal with JP Morgan.

DAY 13:
A Thousand Miles per Gallon

*Society at large always benefits when we find more
efficient modes of producing the goods we desire.*

In today's world, mainstream economic theory comes wrapped,
at virtually every juncture, in politically exploited packages.
The hired henchmen on the left preach the virtues of bigger
government, while those to the right stake their claim (feebly)
to less government and greater personal freedom. Leaving us at
the mercy of a few very bright, academically gifted appointees
who've proven to be most adept at test-taking and, alas, mess-
making.

The fact is that macroeconomics is not nearly as complicated
as many would have us believe. You and I just need to do a
little more outside-the-box thinking and a little more seeing
of the unseen.

A (Hypothetical) Thousand Miles per Gallon
A scientist in Tuscaloosa, in collaboration with his engineer

cousin in Tallahassee, designs the most fuel efficient gas engine known to man: it gets 1,000 miles per gallon. They sell to the Big Three, and over the next decade economic life as we know it improves dramatically. Gas prices plummet, consumer discretionary income soars (creating huge growth and jobs in other industries), tax revenue skyrockets, the government balances its budget, yada yada yada.

But what about the oil industry—what about the workers who'll lose their jobs as demand for oil plummets—shouldn't we somehow protect them? No doubt similar concerns were once voiced on behalf of stagecoach drivers, typists, lamplighters, switchboard operators, milkmen, icemen, copy boys, etc.

You see, while innovation virtually always disrupts a certain labor pool, innovation, without exception, created that pool to begin with.

Bottom line: society at large always benefits when we find more efficient modes of producing the goods we desire.

DAY 14:
Open Wider
(November 2011)

Government is that great fiction, through which everybody endeavors to live at the expense of everybody else.
—Frederic Bastiat

Here are the highlights from Ohio Congressman Dennis Kucinich's rant on Friday (November 11, 2012) evening's edition of CNBC's *Kudlow and Company*—and my translations:

Congressman: "We've got to do something about our trade deficit. We're talking about $550 billion a year; those are jobs out of our country. We've got to start bringing work back into this country."

Translation: We've got to do something about our consumers exploiting the opportunity to save money through international trade. They should pay up for US-made goods. I don't give a rip about the US businesses where the consumer spends that surplus. And forget about those US companies (and the jobs they create) that redeem those US dollars our foreign trading partners are so eager to get their hands on. It's all bad for our unions!

Congressman: "And we've got to prime the pump of our economy."

Translation: And we've got to borrow, tax, and spend more money to keep government growing and our unions going.

Congressman: "If the Fed can create money out of nothing, with its quantitative easing and give it to the banks, or give it to the banks in Europe, why can't our government claim our constitutional authority to be able to create millions of jobs rebuilding America's infrastructure. We should be expanding our economy, we should be creating wealth, we should be creating jobs."

Translation: If the Fed can print money and give it to the banks, why can't we, through tax hikes, higher interest rates, and inflation, suck even more capital out of the private sector to pay for yet another monster spending bill? We need to open the flood gates wider! I have supporters to support!

Congressman: "We need to change our thinking about America and create wealth again and get the government involved in it and stimulating the private sector in a way that everybody wins. This whole approach we're taking right now is a losing approach."

Translation: We need to change our thinking about America and destroy wealth by getting the government involved and stimulate my supporters in a way that only they win. This whole approach we're taking isn't enough … We need bigger government!

Once again, government is that great fiction, through which everybody endeavors to live at the expense of everybody else.

DAY 15:
Q and A on the
Auto Industry Bailout

*When someone in the United States buys a car made in
Japan, somebody in Japan either buys or invests
in something in the United States.*

Q (your everyday consumer) and A (your free-market-
obsessed adviser)—a hypothetical duo illustrating a common
misconception among consumers—are having a discussion. Q
read an article (msnbc.com News Reports, 2012) that claims
the TARP bailout program will net a profit to the taxpayer. As
you'd guess, A has a somewhat different take.

Q: You always bemoan bailouts, but I just read that TARP is
going to net a profit to the taxpayer, and we saved a bunch of
jobs in the process. So I guess the auto industry bailout wasn't
such a bad thing after all, right?

A: Well, let me ask you, if Chrysler had gone out of business in 2008, would folks be buying fewer cars today?

Q: Probably not.

A: So if people wouldn't be buying fewer cars today, would there be fewer US jobs?

Q: Yes, of course there would. While some ex-Chrysler employees would've gone to work for GM and Ford, some of those would've-been-Chrysler buyers would've bought foreign cars. Therefore, some US auto workers would definitely be out of work.

A: So all the would've-been-Chrysler buyers aren't the buy-only-US types? I mean who goes looking for a Chrysler?

Q: What about the Dodge Ram? Or the Jeep Grand Cherokee?

A: Oh, you're right … but there'd still be a bunch that'd go Ford or GM before going Toyota, right?

Q: Yes, but some of that business would still go to Toyota.

A: I agree. So all those new-Toyota-buyers would fly to Japan to buy those cars and trucks?

Q: That's stupid! Of course not! They'd just go to their local Toyota dealership.

A: You mean the dealership owned and run by all those folks Toyota flies in from Japan?

Q: No … my cousin manages a Toyota dealership.

A: Oh, so if demand for Toyota pickups picks up, there might be a few new US jobs created at Toyota dealerships—to replace some of those Chrysler dealer and manufacturing jobs, right?

Q: I guess so …

A: I wonder if there'd be new jobs to be had in Mississippi, Kentucky, Texas, Indiana, Alabama, and West Virginia?

Q: Why just those? There are Toyota dealers in all fifty states.

A: No, I'm talking about Toyota manufacturing plants.

Q: No kidding?

A: No kidding. Toyota has manufacturing plants in all those US states.

Q: I didn't know that …

A: I know you didn't. That's because you knowing that doesn't jibe with protectionist politicking, inspired by the United Auto Workers Union (UAW).

Q: Say what?

A: Those Toyota plants are non-union, and the UAW has huge political influence—and they lobby violently for politicians who'd pay them rents.

Q: What do you mean by "rents"?

A: Have you ever heard the term "rent-seeking"? That's an economist's term for currying political favor, the rents being things like ownership of GM (17.5 percent to their VEBA, an employee benefits trust) and exempting them out of the Affordable Care Act.

Q: That's disgusting!

A: Yep …

Q: But still, we're going to lose some business to Japan.

A: You're right—auto business. But what are those Toyota buyers going to buy those Toyotas with?

Q: Say what?

A: What currency?

Q: Duh! Dollars!

A: And what are those Japanese going to do with those dollars?

Q: Spend them, I suppose.

A: And what can you spend US dollars on?

Q: Huh?

A: US stuff, of course. You see, the only reason Toyota sells us cars is because there's something they want that only US dollars can buy. In essence, when someone in the United States buys a car made in Japan, somebody in Japan either buys or invests in something in the United States—or buys something from somebody else who needs those dollars to buy or invest in something in the United States.

Q: So you're saying jobs would be created in US export industries to offset lost Chrysler jobs?

A: You got it.

Q: I never thought of it that way.

A: You're not supposed to.

Q: How come you didn't mention GM?

A: Because, from what I gather, GM could've filed for bankruptcy much sooner, per the laws (which were broken in the bailout), restructured, and stayed in business right off the bat … Chrysler probably would've had to liquidate.

Q: Oh well … at least folks are still working at Chrysler.

A: Yep, a Chrysler that should be out of business, a Chrysler that was propped up at the expense of American exporters and the consumer at large. That's the government picking winners and losers.

Q: That doesn't sound like capitalism to me.

A: It's not—it's what you call cronyism. And it's a bad thing!

DAY 16:
Gas and Granola
(May 2011)

If we weren't so intolerant of short-term pain, would we be well on the road to recovery by now?

If banks hadn't held back on foreclosures, would we have already seen the bottom in housing?

If Alan Greenspan's Fed hadn't gone hog-wild during the tech bubble-burst, would the real estate bubble and mortgage-backed securities debacle have been averted?

If Ben Bernanke's Fed hadn't gone hog-wilder during the real estate bubble-burst, would the bond market be as bubbly? Would we have averted $4 gas and $400 grocery carts?

If you and five others are stranded on a desert island and you have a granola bar for sale, what's it worth? If your famished fellow castaways have one dollar among them, it's worth a dollar. If they have ten, it's worth ten.

Now, you tell me, when we print trillions, what ultimately happens to the prices of gas and granola? As Milton Friedman said, "Inflation is always and everywhere a monetary phenomenon."

But what if the castaways have ten dollars and you happen to have two granola bars? Well then, they're worth five each. Then, if a chimp steals and eats one, the remaining one, experiencing 100 percent inflation, is worth ten. Now wouldn't that be a supply disruption, as opposed to a monetary phenomenon? Yes, that would be a supply disruption, and a monetary phenomenon. In that the supply of money did indeed increase—on a per-unit basis.

Here's the thing: during recessions, consumer spending declines along with consumer income. Were the economy left to its own devices, prices would descend accordingly. Poorly-run businesses would fail. Well-run businesses would survive—and then thrive as the economy recovers.

If we weren't so intolerant of short-term pain, would we not be well on the road to recovery by now?

DAY 17:
Timely Medicine
(July 2011)

*The beauty of free enterprise is choice; the curse of
central planning is the lack thereof.*

"Next time you need to get here earlier!" was the parting
jab from my airline ticket counter attendant sparring partner
on this too-early Monday morning. What the late-middle-
aged woman with the personality of a menopausal postal clerk
didn't know (or give a rip about) was the frustration a frequent
flier endures while hosing dog diarrhea out of his garage onto
moonlit pavement fifty-five minutes prior to take off.

Rather than share the blow-by-blow with the American
Eagle antagonist (I fear you'd think less of me), I'll vent here
on the virtues of competition (inspired by this morning's
encounter at the ticket counter) and limited government.

The beauty of free enterprise is choice; the curse of central
planning is the lack thereof. I can choose a different airline, but
I can't choose a different DMV. I can choose to max my SEP

IRA contribution, but I can't choose to allocate that 15-plus percent of my income (I'm self-employed) currently confiscated for Social Security to a legitimate retirement plan. The DMV enjoys monopolistic luxury—knowing I've nowhere else to go, they can treat me as they will. As for Social Security—you get the picture.

The ratings agency Moody's suggests that we do away with the whole debt ceiling concept altogether, citing the unnecessary angst it inspires every time it's breached (Brandimarte, 2011). At first blush that sounds pretty darn good. August 2 would be just another day. Just another day, that is, in a year when the world's greatest nation will spend $1.6 trillion more than it brings in. When that nation's debt will exceed $15 trillion (which exceeds its GDP by some $3 trillion). When that nation already sports the second-highest corporate tax rate on the planet. When policymakers conspire to increase regulations on key industries, as well as taxes on job makers (although I am in favor of closing loopholes, along with a lower corporate rate), while their nation's jobless rate pushes 10 percent.

And Moody's would have us do away with this constant reminder of our policymakers' thriftless ways? Nah. As scary (and market-rattling) as the current debt ceiling fiasco may be, I'd say this is timely medicine.

DAY 18:
QE Infinity

We're at the mercy of a few very bright, academically gifted appointees who've proven to be most adept at test-taking and, alas, mess-making.

The Keynesian-minded supporters of QE 1, 2, 3, infinity, and fiscal stimulus (be it payroll tax holidays, cash for clunkers, homebuyers tax credits, unemployment insurance extensions, etc.) would have us believe that the economy struggles because the stimulus programs were insufficient. They would have us believe that we need to step up the volume—and right away. And if we don't, and we double-dip back into recession, insufficient intervention will be the cause.

Like I said in "A Thousand Miles per Gallon," we're at the mercy of a few very bright, academically gifted appointees who've proven to be most adept at test-taking and, alas, mess-making.

George Mason University professor Don Boudreaux

(Boudreaux, 2011), blogging at cafehayek.com, puts it this way:

> It's as if a person who is bleeding to death because of a gunshot wound in his stomach is brought to a physician. The physician correctly realizes that the patient is losing massive amounts of blood and, also, correctly understands that such blood loss is dangerous to the patient's health. So the physician prescribes massive infusions of blood, period. If the patient doesn't recover, the physician orders that the volume of blood-infusions be increased. If the patient dies, the physician will forever blame himself for not increasing the volume of blood-infusions even further. If the patient does recover, the blood-infusions will be praised for saving the patient.

DAY 19:
A Bloat of a Different Color

If I told you you're spending 70 percent more than your annual income, you tell me: Will you be richer or poorer a year from now?

What if I told you you're currently netting, on average, 250 calories per meal more than you're burning off daily? You tell me: Would you be fatter or skinnier a year from now?

If you arrange your daily activities so as to net minimal physical stress, you tell me: Will your bones and muscles be more or less dense, and will they possess more or less capacity a year from now?

What would you say if I told you that you could lose weight by increasing your caloric intake by 70 percent daily? And what if I told you that you could become physically stronger while exerting even less over the next twelve months? As much as you'd love to believe me, you'd tell me I'm full of it.

But what if I were the recipient of the Nobel Prize in nutrition (were there such a thing)? Would you believe me then? Sadly, some of you (those who'd do just about anything not to diet or exercise) would. But alas, my academic prowess notwithstanding, my saying it wouldn't amount to a hill-a-pork-n-beans twelve months from now.

Now what if I told you that you're spending 70 percent more than your annual income? You tell me: Will you be richer or poorer a year from now? And what would you say if I told you that you'd be in better fiscal shape if you spent even more over the next twelve months? I'd be full of it, right?

But what if you were a company? Still full of it. Ah, but what if you were a nation? Now there's a bloat of an entirely different color. For at least one Nobel Prize–winning economist, many other not-Nobel-laureate economists, and oodles of pandering politicians would have you believe that very thing. The question is, do you?

DAY 20:
Guido Says We Have a
Debt Problem
(April 2011)

*All I know is that when a guy named Guido says you have a
debt problem, you, my friend, have a debt problem.*

Ben Bernanke swears that the tools needed to avert the
potential negative side effects of QEs 1 and 2 are at his
disposal. The Republican Congress vows to cut 4 trillion in ten
years; President Obama says it'll take twelve. Unfortunately,
the longer this goes on, the more our leaders sound like the
proverbial gambler begging the mob, on behalf of his kneecaps,
for just a little more time.

All I know is that when a guy named Guido says you have
a debt problem, you, my friend, have a debt problem.

The Group of 20 nations' finance ministers met last
week and unanimously chastised the United States for its
overspending. In the words of Guido Mantega, Brazil's finance

minister, "Ironically, some of the countries that are responsible for the deepest crisis since the Great Depression, and have yet to solve their own problems, are eager to prescribe codes of conduct to the rest of the world." (Central Banking Newsdesk, 2011)

Note: The US's budget deficit looks to hit almost 11 percent of its output in 2011, which ties us for first with Ireland for the highest deficit-to-GDP ratio among developed nations.

Guido makes a good point. And, as I've implied here time and again, our carping about other countries' export incentives and currency policies serve as nothing more than political diversions away from the real issue—which is the egregious mismanagement of our nation's revenue.

DAY 21:

A Very Short List of Government-Related Perverse Incentives

And thus a new industry, rat farming, was born.

In the early 1960s, Europe (attempting to bolster its poultry industry) tariffed US chickens. President Johnson retaliated with a tariff on Europe-made commercial vans. Both tariffs are still on the books. Today, there's a Ford plant in Turkey that affixes rear-side windows and backseats to what would have been commercial vans (i.e., transforming them into consumer, duty free vehicles). They're then shipped to America, where they're stripped of their rear-side windows and backseats (the materials shredded and sent for recycling) and (*voilà!*) become commercial vans. Apparently the above waste costs less than the utterly idiotic tax.

When teachers are rewarded for their students' improved test scores, do we get more effective teachers and better-educated kids or more effective test-teachers and better test-takers? When teachers are rewarded for student evaluation scores, do we get better teachers or easier courses and inflated grades?

Government can indeed create industry. For example, in Hanoi, under French colonial rule, they had a rat problem. Therefore, in its infinite wisdom, the government instituted a program where folks were paid bounties for rat pelts. And thus a new industry, rat farming, was born.

Would a farmer who comes across a chartreuse-spotted salamander immediately contact the Fish and Wildlife Service? Or would he engage in "preemptive habitat destruction" (with a shovel) over fear he'd lose the use of his land due to the Endangered Species Act?

Ask yourself, honestly, if unemployment benefits ended at twenty-six weeks, like they used to, would the long-term unemployed be unemployed so long-term?

When government mandates mileage standards for new automobiles, meaning you get more miles per gallon, will you be nearly as odometerphobic? In other words, as driving gets cheaper, would traffic get denser (more drivers, more traffic jams, more roads, more cars, more pollution)?

My point being, well intended or not, government intrusion into the marketplace all too often results in distorted pricing, incentives gone awry, and unintended negative consequences.

DAY 22:

Throwing Money at Problems Caused by Throwing Money at Problems

We don't like pain any more than politicians do.

Ask yourself, who would sign on to run a company where he'd have to answer to a board made up of ardent supporters on one side of the table and individuals committed to making certain he does not receive a second employment contract on the other?

And let's say that company was in a state of utter fiscal disaster and that, given the makeup of the board, there was virtually no chance that this executive could measurably turn things around during the course of his first employment contract. Also, the pay for running this bloody behemoth doesn't come near what he earns currently.

In summary, this new job would subject him and his family to unrelenting and vicious attacks, an utterly palpable sense of futility, a virtual no-win scenario, and a huge cut in pay.

So who would want to be elected or reelected President? A politician is a special kind of person. Egomania is *the* requisite, along with the strongest will to succeed to two full terms. All this leads to policy decisions aimed at placating the populace over very short periods—that is, throwing money at problems that were caused by throwing money at problems.

That, my friends, is the fundamental "problem" in the world today. But alas, that's the nature of politics, and life— people pursuing their own separate objectives. We simply have to train our officials better. We have to teach them that it is in their best interest to make better policy decisions.

Is that a pipe dream? Of course it is! We don't like pain any more than politicians do.

So here's how this plays out: The patient (the economy) ultimately heals itself, by the grace of its immune system (the entrepreneurial spirit), and grows us out of this predicament, albeit much more slowly than it would have without all the intervention. And the politicians and Fed officials will take all the credit.

DAY 23:

Freshman Economics

*If your food's the best, your customers
will keep coming back.*

It's the day after the president's jobs speech (September 10, 2011), and I'm picking up my ninth grader and his buddy from school. I say to them, "Dudes, I have a question for you: Let's say you own one of the top two restaurants in town, and are in need of a cook. Three people apply.

There's John; he's one of the area's best chefs and currently works for the other one of the top two. Then there's Jane, who recently lost her first chef's job due to her employer going out of business. Their food was—uh, well, they're out of business. And lastly there's Jim, who just got laid off at another local restaurant. They say he's a pretty good chef, but, well, he got laid off.

So whom do you hire?"

They, without hesitation and in unison, reply, "John." I say, "Good answer. But what if I told you that Jane's been unemployed for seven months, and Jim's a veteran. Which, in either case, would win you a very nice, one-time, several-thousand-dollar tax break? Now whom do you hire?"

With a half-second hesitation and in unison, they reply, "John" (not at all concerned with the tax credit). I say, "Why?" My son's friend answers, "If your food's the best, your customers will keep coming back. You'll make a lot more money that way."

I then ask, "So what if you didn't need a new cook, but the government was going to give you a big chunk of money for hiring one anyway (if he or she's a vet or has been unemployed for six-plus months). Would you?" Without hesitation, they reply in unison, "No" (a smirky teenager, that's-a-stupid-question kind of no). Asking why would have been an intellectual insult and inspired more smirkiness, so I don't.

So how is it that a couple of high school freshmen have better business sense than the authors of the president's jobs bill? Clear is the mind unpolluted by politics.

DAY 24:
Freshman Economics Part 2 (September 2011)

That, ladies and gentlemen, is how we end up $16 trillion in debt.

Had another one of those teenager carpooling moments yesterday. Not only do my son's buddies now hop in expecting an econ lesson; they're beginning to come with their own topics. Yesterday, Robbie starts with, "What's going on with the market?" After my pithy response (I find kids get almost any concept as long as I throw in a few "dudes" and make references to their weekly allowance), he asks if I heard about some conference in Washington where the government paid $16 each for the muffins and $6 for every cup of coffee.

I say, "Here's the problem, Robbie. As a very wise gentleman used to say, there are four ways you spend money."

My boy Ryan chimes in here and says, "Dad, Dad, let me say the last one!" (I guess he's heard this a time or two).

I say: "Number one. You spend your own money on

yourself. You'll be careful how much you spend and you'll make sure you get your money's worth.

"Number two. You spend your own money on someone else. You'll be careful how much you spend but you won't be quite so concerned with quality.

"Number three. You spend someone else's money on yourself. You won't be as careful how much you spend, but you'll make sure you get their money's worth."

Ryan says, "Number four is when you spend someone else's money on someone else. You spend all you want and you don't care what you get."

I close with "Number four, Robbie, is government. And that is how they end up spending $16 for a muffin." (Although this one might be a number three, depending on who ordered the muffins).

And that, ladies and gentlemen, is how we end up $16 trillion in debt. (Note: credit for the four ways we spend money goes to the late Milton Friedman (Ross 2011).

DAY 25:
The Manufacturing Evolution
(January 2012)

Government picking winners is cronyism by definition.

A Republican hopeful, during last week's CNN candidates' debate, attempted to make the case for a zero corporate tax rate for the manufacturing industry and 17.5 percent for everybody else. He stated that the cost of doing business in the United States makes manufacturing goods more expensive, versus our overseas competition.

Notwithstanding his noble intentions, government picking winners (favoring one industry over another) is cronyism by definition. And that's where we get into trouble. If you give preferential tax treatment to one industry, make no mistake, others will lobby hard to convince you that they are every bit as critical to the growth of jobs in this country (or, sinisterly speaking, that they will more strenuously promote your ambitions). Net result: more companies devoting more resources to lobbying Washington and less to expansion (jobs), etc.

There's forever an evolutionary process with regard to manufacturing, involving gains in technology and the movement of production to wherever cheap and efficient labor resides. And, trust me, that's precisely how it should be. Take Hong Kong, for example: After World War II, Hong Kong quickly became an export-driven manufacturing center. During the ensuing years, however, it underwent a nearly 100 percent transition to a service-based economy. And today boasts one of the most robust economies on the planet.

The following sentence taken from the Economic Freedom Index website's summary of the Hong Kong economy (Hong Kong 2012) says it all: "Regulatory efficiency and openness to global commerce strongly support entrepreneurial dynamism, while overall macroeconomic stability minimizes uncertainty."

I suspect that regulatory inefficiency (and its attendant uncertainty) has much to do with the United States' anything-but-robust economy of late, as well as its plunge from number 3 to number 10 on the Economic Freedom Index. Hong Kong, by the way, ranks number 1 (Economic Freedom Index 2012).

DAY 26:
The City Discriminates against Teens and the Unskilled

When we're talking basic economics, politicians are either profoundly ignorant, or they assume we are.

You'd think that San Francisco would be the last place you'd find blatant discrimination against the young and the undertrained. But there's no denying this one: effective January 1, 2012, the City ~~By the Bay~~ Where You Pay bumped its minimum wage to $10.24 an hour—making it the only city in America to breach the $10 mark, and the toughest place for a kid to get a job.

I didn't even know this until I heard yesterday that San Franciscans will now have to pay up (consequently) for the **Subway** ~~$5~~ Footlong. Going forward, $5 will only buy you 9.74 inches of sandwich. The new jingle, "Five dollar half-a-foot plus three-and-three-quarter-inch long," just doesn't stick in your brain like the old "five-dollar footlong" did.

But that's the way of it folks. When we're talking basic

economics, politicians are either profoundly ignorant, or they assume we are. Here's Walter Williams (Williams, 2003) on forced minimums:

> Minimum prices in general tend to discriminate against the lesser skilled person or the less preferred item. Let's say ten workers show up and you only can hire five. Well, you can't discriminate based on price because you have to pay them all eight dollars an hour. So you may hire according to what you like. So if you prefer Catholics to Jews or whites to blacks, you'll have a tendency to indulge your preferences. You can apply that phenomena to anything. If we made a law, let's call it a "minimum steak law," that is, fillet mignon and chuck steak both sell for $10. Well, the cost of discriminating against chuck steak would be zero, because you have to pay $10 anyway. The way that less preferred things compete with more preferred things is by having a lower price. Even though people prefer filet mignon to chuck steak, chuck steak doesn't have any problems selling at all.

DAY 27:

Good Grief!
Where Are All the Jobs?
(October 2009)

*Isn't it just a little embarrassing that the greatest
country in the world is running monster deficits
and piling up debt faster than a nineteen-year-old
with a MasterCard and an Internet connection?*

It's amazing: the economy hasn't even (officially) stopped receding and we're already hearing that familiar chorus: "Where are all the jobs?" And, as usual, the choir consists primarily of those who would gain politically from a less than stellar recovery. That very same refrain was sung from the opposite side of the aisle as we came out of the 2002 recession.

The bad news for today's cynical sopranos is that all (make that most) indicators are pointing to positive GDP growth for the third quarter. They will find their support, however, in the fact that while the economy is about to move into expansion mode, we have about as much chance of seeing a near-term improvement in employment as Linus has of seeing the Great Pumpkin this Halloween.

Here's the thing: job growth rarely occurs in the early stages of an economic recovery. I mean, good grief! Half the country's companies have just laid off half their workforce— do you suppose they'll be hiring anytime soon? And besides, the tech sector has remained hard at work inventing all kinds of new stuff designed to make companies more efficient. That is, if the new computer application makes businesses more productive (which will ultimately result in more, and better, jobs) and doesn't require health insurance and a pension, it's going to be awhile before they (save for the tech sector) even glance at any new job applications.

So while the critics play the "no jobs" tune like Schroeder plays Beethoven, don't fret over the near-term continued weak employment stats. Again, that's pretty much the norm. But what's not the norm, and what honestly concerns me, is the fact that recent fiscal policy hasn't been entirely consistent with what you might expect given the depth of this recession. One would think that since policymakers forever see policy as the answer, we'd be looking forward to things like capital gains and business tax cuts—things that might inspire the private sector to expand and create jobs—as opposed to things like healthcare reform, raising tax rates on businesses, financial industry regulatory reform (FINREG), and the like.

With regard to healthcare reform, I understand the talking point: "It's an embarrassment that the greatest country in the world has so many uninsured citizens." Not to discount that by any means, but isn't it just a little embarrassing that the greatest country in the world is running monster deficits and piling up debt faster than a nineteen-year-old with a MasterCard and an Internet connection? This is clearly not the time to embark upon such ambitious and, sadly, ambiguous legislation. I know, I digress.

Getting back to job growth: to be fair, there are government programs afoot designed specifically to produce new jobs, as we pave some roads and build a bridge or two. But when employment is created for the sake of employment itself, the jobs we get will in no way reflect free-market demand. Sure, we'll see the construction projects and think, "Ah, that's great, our tax dollars are putting people back to work," but we won't see the legitimate, longer-lasting jobs that weren't created (or worse yet, lost) because those dollars were extracted from the real economy.

DAY 28:
Pain Is Essential

Simply put: pain in life, and in business, is essential.

In Ayn Rand's book *The Virtue of Selfishness* (Rand & Branden 1964), she made brief reference to people with a rare condition that renders them insensitive to pain. My immediate thought upon reading her reference was how such a condition might be analogous to the players in the 2008 credit crisis. So I did a little research. And while it was easy to make my point in the following, I must say that the articles I read and the videos I watched on congenital insensitivity to pain with anhidrosis syndrome (CIPA) were anything but easy to take in; in fact, they were utterly heartbreaking. There are precious children in this world (seldom surviving childhood) who are otherwise as vibrant and beautiful as children can be who literally feel no physical pain. I would never have imagined how truly tragic this turns out to be.

Pain Is Essential

How would you like to be one of the few hundred people in the world who live literally pain free? Never to experience a headache, a bad back, or pulled muscle. Never to need a pain pill, not even an aspirin. To never suffer the aches of an aging body. Think about it: the sheer bliss. The excitement. What would you try? What risks would you take, knowing you'd feel no physical pain?

How would you like to have been a CEO of a major Wall Street firm at virtually anytime over the past thirty years? Your senses numbed by the knowledge that Uncle Sam would steal away your pain if you banged your head too hard. Knowing you could lever-up to unheard-of multiples and never truly lose. Stay in business, get your bonus, pay the staff at your Swiss chalet—or, at the very worst, walk away with a few dozen (if not a few hundred) million, while the taxpayer buys the mistakes off your firm's balance sheet. Leaving you, or your successors, with billions of crisp new dollars with which to leverage the next bets. My, the risks you would take.

Better to have been the latter. For while the notion of never feeling physical pain may, at first blush, seem amazing, the lives of children with congenital insensitivity to pain with anhidrosis (CIPA) are anything but. Their fingertips are missing, their tongues are mangled, they get heatstroke often (they don't sweat), fractured bones go unnoticed, and, tragically, their lifespans are shortened. Parents of the CIPA child never rest. They can't turn their backs for a second, for there's no physical limit to the harm their child might inflict, unwittingly, upon himself.

As for the Wall Street exec of 2008, he maintains ten finely manicured fingertips and suffers zero fractured bones.

Not that his reckless actions didn't inflict great pain; on the contrary, they did indeed—just not, alas, onto himself. The unavoidable (natural) consequences of his egregious risk-taking and overleveraging were relegated, at the hands of politicians and central bankers, to the taxpayer.

As for the moral hazard of bailouts: they'd have us believe that with all the new regulations, too-big-to-fail is no longer a possibility—that, like the CIPA parent, Washington has Wall Street under strict surveillance. But make no mistake: mistakes will be made. As long as we persist in appointing career politicians concerned with merely the immediate term (their term in office, that is), Washington will crony-up to corporate America, unions, etc., and vice versa.

Simply put: pain in life, and in business, is essential.

DAY 29:
The Chicken Came First

A culture of dependency, once established, is virtually (politically) impossible to reverse.

One could argue that government stimulus programs, including unemployment insurance extensions, resulted in greater iPhone sales over the past three years than otherwise would have occurred. Therefore the theory (Keynesianism) that promotes government intervention (to boost consumption) as the best method of aiding a weak economy has indeed been proven. Right?

Question: Was there demand for cell phones before the first one was produced? Were consumers lined up outside Ma Bell's door at the crack of every dawn to get first crack at the first mobile phone? Or was it the foresight of some genius and the audacity (and capital) of some tech firm that brought the first cell phone to market?

The age-old debate, supply-side vs. demand-side economics, rages on. Those who would advocate government intervention—through deficit spending—during an economic contraction make the logical (at first blush) case that handing out money to the populace stimulates consumption, which stimulates production, which stimulates employment, which stimulates the economy back into growth mode.

Those of us who would advocate no new spending programs, but rather, if anything (nothing might be better), producer incentives such as lower corporate and capital gains tax rates, make the case that the chicken indeed precedes the egg. That if budget deficits during economic contractions are to be exacerbated by policy, that they should occur not as a result of increased government spending—creating a culture of dependency that, once established, is virtually (politically) impossible to reverse—but as a result of leaving more capital in the hands of forward-thinking entrepreneurs.

DAY 30:

Political Chicken
(December 2012)

Your man in office got there by making all the right promises to all the right people.

Yesterday, senators Harry Reid and Mitch McConnell delivered their speeches. Reid "can't imagine their (the house Republicans) consciences". McConnell reports telling the President that "this is a conversation we should have had months ago" (Karl & Miller, 2012)—implying that the President's aloofness is to blame for this dancing on the edge of the "fiscal cliff". Essentially, they each spent their floor time chastising the opposing party.

If you lean left, Reid was right on the money. If you lean right, McConnell was simply stating the facts. If you understand that the actors who sit on both sides of the aisle are, first and foremost, concerned with the political ramifications of this fix they've gotten themselves into, you realize that what we're witnessing is nothing more than a game of political chicken. And in the game of chicken, the flinching generally occurs a second or two before the would've-been collision. Hence, here we are on December 28th.

If you haven't come to this realization (what truly motivates politicians), then you sincerely believe that these men and women who we've deposited onto Washington—the ones who sit on the side you lean to that is—have the character and fortitude to put the nation's best interest ahead of their own. Hmm...

Now think about it. Think about running for office. Think about what it would take to get yourself elected to the Senate. For starters, it would take some serious money to fund your campaign. So you'll be fundraising. And who would offer up the cash necessary to promote your ambition? John Dillinger said he robbed banks "because that's where the money is". Now if being a bank robber was a requisite for holding public office, a bank robber your man would be. But since illegally stealing other people's money lands one in a U.S. penitentiary, as opposed to the U.S. Senate, he had to resort to less extreme measures, like asking bank and other industries' executives—and other interested parties with money—for donations in return for promises to legally steal taxpayer money (to subsidize his supporters' aims) once in office.

Let's say that you're a different sort of candidate, you're honest. And that you're an advocate for limited government, a free-market ideologue. You understand that government subsidies are nothing more than methods of redistributing taxpayer money to politically favored industries. So you vow to put an end to corporate welfare. Now how much money do you suspect you'll raise from CEOs? You got it, zip!

Ah, but then the general public, $25 at a time, will fund

your campaign. Well, the thing is, you recognize that Social Security, Medicare and Medicaid present unfunded liabilities to the tune of some $85 trillion, and, therefore, serious reform—which you vow to undertake—is needed. And you understand that being unemployed, while still no picnic, is less painful today than it's ever been. And, therefore, knowing that you get what you pay for (that is, extend unemployment benefits and you extend unemployment) you'll push for the ending of unemployment benefit extensions. And you feel the welfare system is doing little more than perpetuating its own existence. Now how much do you suspect, at twenty-five bucks a pop, you'll raise from the general public? You got it, zip!

Ah, but you're a gazillionaire. You can fund your own campaign—you don't need to kowtow to any special interest. Okay, but remember, you can't simply buy your way into office—somebody's got to vote for you.

So here's the thing: Your man in office got there by making all the right promises to all the right people. Promises that public policy would be tilted in his supporters' favor. Like it or not, that's the path to public office. And that is *the* single reason we are where we are. Our "leaders" are weighing the political ramifications of the short-term economic ramifications of whatever they'll ultimately sign onto. As for potential long-term economic ramifications, well, they're hoping those will land on someone else's watch.

DAY 31:
Products of Our Environment

The measure of one's intellect is no match for one's predisposition.

With bent brow he peers above wire-rimmed spectacles resting near the tip of his nose, his gaze descending upon three dozen young frontal-lobe-underdeveloped college freshmen. With blatant contempt for the values that built a great nation and provided him a platform to stand above the impressionable, the pretentious PhD addresses his barely post-adolescent pupils. With incomparable eloquence he marvels the lower-classmen. His charge is to teach, his objective to impeach. To impeach a commoner's allegiance to his country, to a flag dressed in stars and stripes. He exposes capitalism for how he sees it—a system of selfishness, of ruthless abandon, of obscene opulence. There are no subtleties in his reproach.

He offers up the life of one William Gates, the near-wealthiest man on earth and the product of the dark-sided capitalism. He implores his students to consider his rhetorical query: "How can we allow a single human being to earn literally hundreds of millions of dollars in a single year while others toil for a workman's wage?" Lacking sufficient knowledge, or courage, not a student would challenge the pompous professor.

Later that evening, as my then eighteen-year-old son shared his story, I was amazed to find that I could actually feel my pulse pounding from within my eyeballs. While I was fully aware that my offspring would encounter ideologies that wouldn't always jibe with the teachings of his old man, I was nonetheless taken aback that this econ professor would dare exploit his position to promote his warped ideology.

I proceeded to equip my son with the obvious retorts, such as, "How can we allow a college professor to knock down six figures when we have kindergarten teachers working their bottoms off for less than half that amount?"

I was considering how I might personally lambast the conceited collectivist for imposing his personal agenda onto my young son and his classmates when the obvious occurred to me: there was no way I nor anyone else would change this sadly misguided individual's mind or how he addresses his students. And besides, he's just an unfortunate product of his environment—perhaps a disciple of one of his own college instructors. Challenging him directly or petitioning for his dismissal for pushing his politics would be a profound waste of time and energy. In fact, in a way, I'm kind of glad he's there. In the case of my son, he's learning that ignorance is ignorance, even when it's well-credentialed and dressed in fine eloquence.

Of course I've nothing to worry about; Nick is an independent-thinking, proud-to-be-a-capitalist young man.

Either that or he is, in the certain opinion of any passionate socialist, a product of his environment—a disciple of a delusional free-market-capitalist father. And I'm okay with that.

So I, the capitalist whacko, think the socialist professor is nothing more than an extension of his ideological upbringing, and he would think the same of me. And you know, maybe we're both right—perhaps we are each, when it comes to our politics, largely products of our environment. And to be perfectly honest, while I'm no psychologist, I do believe that to be the case. In fact I'm reasonably certain this condition afflicts virtually all walks of people—and trust me; the measure of one's intellect is no match for one's predisposition. Years spent at our nation's greatest universities can be practically wasted, for when the academic emerges, his insight into the world at large is first and foremost filtered through the political veil that has been engrained into his very being. Therefore, in the case of my son's teacher, again, there's absolutely no changing his mind. And the same goes for me. There's absolutely nothing that will change my belief in free-market capitalism.

CONCLUSION

In the opinion of the proctor in my Day 31 essay, the United States is heading down a path of destruction, which, by the way, is what I hear regularly from some of my capitalist-minded brethren as well. The distinction being that the collectivist-minded professor believes capitalism will be our doom, while the capitalist fears we're heading toward a socialistic dead-end. And while I'd expect such cynicism from the professor, I'm always a bit surprised when I hear it from one of my patriotic pals.

Truly, to suggest that this great country's entrepreneurial foundation, having survived all that the past two-and-a-quarter-plus centuries could dish out, can't survive a political term or two is, quite frankly, preposterous. Yet, all too often, I hear those who would profess their faith in the American way brood on as if the next piece of legislation will spell our demise.

So with all due respect, if you have found yourself complaining in a similar fashion, while I understand your concern, you have got to be kidding me! Of course this is just me filtering the world through my environmentally influenced ideology. And you know—I'm okay with that.

It is my sincerest hope that the past month has brought you some insight into how the political process impacts the economy. While at times things may seem hopeless, while indeed the pendulum will continue to swing between ideologies, I believe there's a bright future in store for the free-market ideal—I suspect I'll be publishing more on the subject in the years to come. In the meantime you'll find volumes on my blog, www.betweenthelines.us.

BIBLIOGRAPHY

Boffey, L. C. (2012, March 12). "A Moment of Truth for Health Care Reform," *New York Times*, p. 1.

Boudreaux, D. (2011, August 1). "Bloody Keynesians." Retrieved August 1, 2011, from Cafe Hayek. http://cafehayek.com/2011/08/bloody-keynesians.html.

Brandimarte, W. (2011, July 18). "Moody's Suggests US Eliminate Debt Ceiling." Retrieved July 2011 from Reuters. http://www.reuters.com/article/2011/07/18/us-usa-debt-moodys-idUSTRE76H0WH20110718.

Buchanan, J. (n.d.). *The Consise Encyclopedia of Economics*. Retrieved June 9, 2012, from Library of Economics and Liberty. http://www.econlib.org/library/Enc/bios/Buchanan.html.

Central Banking Newsdesk (2011, April 18). "Brazil Slams IMF Proposal on Capital Controls." Retrieved October 3, 2012, from Central Banking.com. http://www.centralbanking.com/central-banking/news/2044465/brazil-slams-imf-proposal-capital-controls.

Dash, E. (2012, November 13). Banks Quietly Ramping Up Costs to Consumers. *New York Times*, p. 2.

Economic Freedom Index (2012). Retrieved January 23, 2012, from Heritage.org. www.heritage.org/index/default.

Hong Kong (2012). Retrieved January 23, 2012, from Heritage. org. www.heritage.org/index/country/hongkong.

Karl, J., & Miller, S. (2012, December 27). *White House Says It Has No New Fiscal Cliff Plan*. Retrieved December 28, 2012, from abcnews.go.com: http://abcnews.go.com /Politics/OTUS/white-house-fiscal-cliff-plan/story?id= 18075505#.UOyK9W-5Msd

Keynes, J. M. (1936/2009). *The General Theory of Employment, Interest, and Money.* New York: Classic Books America.

Levitt, S. D., and S. J. Dubner (2005). *Freakonomics.* New York: Harper Perrenial.

Market Watch (2011, July 10). *Italian sell-off prompts emergency euro zone meet.* Retrieved October 8, 2012, from Market Watch. http://articles.marketwatch.com/2011-07-10/ economy/30808295_1_greek-bailout-european-central-bank-italian-government-bond-yields.

msnbc.com news reports. (2012, April 13). "Taxpayers to Make Money on TARP, Treasury Says." Retrieved April 13, 2012, from The Bottom Line on msnbc.com. http://bottomline. msnbc.msn.com/_news/2012/04/13/11186623-taxpayers-to-make-money-on-tarp-treasury-says?lite.

Rand, A., and N. Branden (1964). "The Virtue of Selfishness," in A. Rand and N. Branden, *The Virtue of Selfishness.* New York: New American Library.

Reuters (2012, May 11). "JPMorgan Hit by 'Egregious' Trading Loss of $2 Billion." Retrieved 2012 йил 11-May from CNBC.com. http://www.cnbc.com/id/47377555/.

Ross, R (2011, October 5). *Friedman's Four Ways.* Retrieved June 8, 2012, from The American Spectator: http://spectator.org/archives/2011/10/05/friedmans-four-ways/print.

Sanati, C. (2012, January 26). Retrieved October 2, 2012, from CNN Money. http://finance.fortune.cnn.com/2012/01/26/bank-of-america-turnaround/.

Smith, A. (1786). "The Wealth of Nations," in A. Smith, *An Inquiry into the Nature and Causes of The Wealth of Nations (facsimile of the edition published in 1786).* Adamant Media Corporation.

Sullivan, A. (2003). *Economics: Principles in Action.* Upper Saddle River: Pearson Prentice Hall.

US Treasury Press Center (2011, March 30). "TARP Bank Programs Turn Profit after Three Financial Institutions Repay $7.4 Billion." Retrieved October 9, 2012, from US Department of the Treasury. http://www.treasury.gov/press-center/press-releases/Pages/tg1121.aspx.

Williams, W. (2003, November 7). "Considerable Quotes." Retrieved June 9, 2012, from Considerable Quotes. http://www.thepaytons.org/essays/quotes/2003_11_01_archive.html.

ABOUT THE AUTHOR

Martin Mazorra, a Certified Financial Planner and Chartered Financial Consultant, is co-founder of Private Wealth Advisors, LLC in Fresno, California. He is the author of *Making Lemonade, A Bright View on Investing, on Financial Markets and on the Economy*. He and his wife, Judy, have five incredible children and three beautiful grandchildren.